WINTHROPOS

WINTHROPOS

POEMS

GEORGE KALOGERIS

LOUISIANA STATE UNIVERSITY PRESS

BATON ROUGE

Published by Louisiana State University Press
lsupress.org

LSU Press Paperback Original

Designer: Laura Roubique Gleason
Typeface: MinionPro

Cover photograph: Getty Images/iStockphoto, Toltek

Library of Congress Cataloging-in-Publication Data

Names: Kalogeris, George, author.
Title: Winthropos : poems / George Kalogeris.
Description: Baton Rouge : Louisiana State University Press, [2021]
Identifiers: LCCN 2020054207 (print) | LCCN 2020054208 (ebook) |
    ISBN 978-0-8071-7567-5 (paperback) | ISBN 978-0-8071-7599-6 (pdf) |
    ISBN 978-0-8071-7600-9 (epub)
Subjects: LCGFT: Poetry
Classification: LCC PS3611.A454 W56 2021 (print) | LCC PS3611.A45
    (ebook) | DDC 811/.6—dc23
LC record available at https://lccn.loc.gov/2020054207
LC ebook record available at https://lccn.loc.gov/2020054208

For John and Irene
And for Richard Fein and David Ferry

CONTENTS

IV

V

VI

WINTHROPOS

WINTHROPOS

And if you get lost, Yorgáki, what will you do?
"I'll find some older people and tell them my name."
Anything else? "I'll tell them where I live."

And where is that? "Forty-five Locust Ave."
And where is that? "Winthrop." Then comes his vague,
Winthrop, Yorgáki? Or is it Winthropos . . .

Only now that I'm older than he ever was,
And even in late middle age wherever I am
In my life I still don't have the foggiest clue,

Do I hear the rhyme. Obvious, unavoidable.
It tells me the answer to the Sphinx's riddle
Is *Anthropos.* My father pulling my leg.

TALKING TO MYSELF ABOUT POETRY

Whatever you do, do not give up on it.
Keep listening for someone walking behind you—
However faint those footfalls they're not unheard.

Trust that your language, lost in the *deep dark wood*
Of your larynx, will find another poet's guidance
To read you back to yourself, and break the silence.

Just saying: "My heart was in my mouth, Meroúla"
Sings back the nightingale in your mother's voice.
Whatever you do, do not give up on it.

At the end of another day with the page still blank
Yet the low horizon ablaze like consummate art,
Who doesn't believe their lines aren't worth a straw?

Nobody. Dream on, Nobody. At the end of the day,
Ocean still echoes in earshot of open shells.
Rosy-fingered dawn is under your eyelids.

So your words are dead to the world. Let them lie there
True to themselves. As far from the teeming swarming
Inconceivable hives of Mount Hyméttus

The poem to come may seem, just one not too
Mellifluous hum and there they are, the lyric
Honeybees. It may be tonight they glaze

Your sleeping lips with honey of Mount Hyméttus.
Dream on like disillusioned sweetly intoning
Antonio Machado: music for a mule

Pulling a waterwheel in a dusty circle.
Dream on. You are a tired animal
With blinders on, but nothing is clearer than water

Rising and falling in Andalusian song.
Remember that Poetry was there for you
In your darkest hour, that *noche oscura* when you

Were twenty-four, and suddenly fatherless.
It's when you started writing verse, in earnest.
Whatever you do, do not give up on it.

Keep reading Seamus Heaney and Juan de la Cruz.

BABY MONITOR

She's sound asleep. Or her Alzheimer's is. I can hear
Each breath she takes through the monitor I keep
On my desk, hooked up as it is to the one upstairs,

Beside her bed. The kind of listening
Device that's used for keeping track of infants.
The tremulous speaker could fit in the palm of your hand.

A little green light pulses every time
It picks up any trace of my mother's voice.
Babble of baby talk and muffled whimpers.

Those garbled bits expelled from her speech machine,
Its plastic speaker propped all night on its stand,
Calling out softly some rhythmical ruminant something

So automatic it might be dreaming out loud,
In my mother's oblivious voice—O Sibylline
Machine that makes the incomprehensible clear:

"... and please help her ... and please guide him ... and stop
It from spreading to the kidneys, please, dear Lord ...
And make that enough to meet their mortgage payments ..."

I'm privy to a prayer that no one else
Can hear. At least tonight. Some primal psalm
Where all are nameless, but none of them forgotten.

And *please* and *please* and *please* goes the little green pulsing light.

VEIL

Caught in a sun-shower on my way to school,
I once took shelter by ducking under a willow.
Its branches hung down so low they swept the street.

I was stepping through beaded curtains, thick as catkins.
The rainwater glittered running down the vines.
My books in their slung green satchel stirred like seedlings.

Black earth. Moist roots. The bole-mouth oozing tar . . .
I could have waited things out in the candy store,
But I was shy. I was a firstborn. For years

I never knew why those elderly relatives
Would look at me that way. They spoke no English.
Their coats were heavy. Whatever they'd been through

I stepped back out from under the veil of the willow
Just as the dew was shining on everything:
The houses, the sidewalk. Even the dark Atlantic.

PEPONIA

Honeydew melons, swelling their shipping crates,
Kept cool in the damp cellar dark of my father's store:

Out of sight but never so far out of mind
That every so often a crowbar's iron talon

Couldn't pry open their plywood lids, suspending
The nails like fangs. If ripeness is all, it was all

In the way I saw the way my father cradled
Pepónia, turning them over slowly enough

To keep the luminous pallor of their moist
Complexions fresh: still bright in the long look back

Through the cellar dark. All in the way he'd never
Say what he saw, but set them gently back down

In their wooden crates. Then every so often another
Aura would hover there, in the afterglow

Of a dangling bulb's interrogating glare.
Which still can make my father's sisters appear,

Crouching together before a crumbling wall.
I mean in that black-and-white snapshot my mother kept

On her perfumed dresser, with its oval mirror.
And those open, kerchiefed faces staring back

From the open fields, late in the nineteen thirties.
As if a crowbar angled into the dark

Were leverage enough to release the fragrant, opulent
Sheen of those who never cross over the water

But hover near whenever I say *pepónia*:
Honeydew melons, swelling their shipping crates.

READING ZH

I was lying in bed and reading Herbert's poems
(The Polish Herbert) when I heard the man say:

"You hear the machine gun because I open the window"—
I mean the one whose house was under siege

In Syria, but whose voice had entered my room
Through the radio on my nightstand. It was late,

And it was Herbert's poetry speaking to me
As I read his Warsaw poem about the girl

Dissecting a lyric poem in the library.
With her sharpened pencil she marks the lines with slashes

To show the stresses, until each scrupulous verse,
For all its unflinching ardor, now resembles

"A salamander the ants are swarming over."
Before the poet could witness the death of his words,

Zbigniew Herbert says, his bleeding body
Was dragged away under heavy fire.

As I count the beats of this iambic line,
Phoebus Apollo is flaying Marsyas alive.

Way out west the sunlit stump of a giant
Sequoia has rings inscribed with dates that radiate

Out from the redwood's core, as if that stump
Was living proof of the Annals of Tacitus,

The Chronicles of the Crusades, Columbus's log . . .
When I close the book of poems, I put out the light.

In the afterglow of its shade, the lamp hovers
Like goose-necked Nike, the goddess who hesitates.

Then everything goes black as a smoldering campsite.
"You hear the machine gun because I open the window,"

Said the man whose house was under siege.
Those riddled by disaster are always alone.

Suspended outside my window, the billowing dark
Occludes the lamp of the moon—but it's still there,

Aglow inside the clouds, like a backlit grotto
Of frozen lava. Old Masters are painting the night

As they always do: suffused with ashen sfumato.

LETHE

In the spotless hospice I visit my Uncle Charlie,
The one who had English, and last of my father's siblings

To leave their village. A wall-mounted TV plays
Without any sound. My uncle's so weak he can't speak.

When he's asked to sip some juice through a straw, it only
Goes halfway up, then flows back into the cup,

Away from his lips. He closes his eyes in relief.
Now I squeeze his hand; now he bows his head; and kisses

The back of my wrist. Then headlong back to oblivion's
Blankness sinks, on pillows. A kiss so resigned,

So fervently parched, you'd think he met the Pope.
Or was like old Priam beseeching the great Achilles.

My uncle, although not yet one of Pluto's shades—
His lips are moving there, in the speechless dark.

He bows his head and kisses my writing hand
Again, in a dream. His bloodless lips won't let me

Forget how it tastes, down there, to him, *bereft*.

WEIGHING GRAPES

Before it was empty again, and over your head,
Before the arrow swung all the way back to zero,
There they were, in a platter fit for Nero:
Two pounds of grapes. When I was small enough,
And that was just enough, for the dipping pan
To hold me in sway, eye-level with all those lucid,
Opaque rinds of iridescence: *Emerald*
Concords, Ruby Niagaras, Flame Tokays—
And some other kind as pale as frosted berries.

Though just the same, to us they were all *stafýlia*:
Grapes to be weighed and bagged on Saturday mornings.
Back when the wild Dionysian Sixties were only
Beginning their strange unfurling, *stafýlia* were shining
Between the slats of plywood crates. As if
The term itself was one more thing for us
To unpack, in Greek, at Winthrop Quality Market.
Cluster by cluster they glittered from my fingers,
Like jewelry out of a chest of buried treasure—

At least that's how I passed them to Uncle Charlie,
Whose waiting hands were just as jittery as
The dangling pan he was heaping with grapes. No matter
How lightly he set them down, or lifted them out,
The spring-bolt arrow shot wildly back and forth
Across the dial, and like a nervous tic
It never really settled. That shaky pan.
My wary, immigrant uncle. As if he knew
There was always some invisible thumb on the scale.

Emerald Concords, Ruby Niagaras, Flame
Tokays . . . Oswald and Ruby . . . Athenian tanks
Treading on Syntagma Square . . . Whatever hangs
In the balance, and always comes in clusters, for me
It starts with *stafýlia*. Grapes like the grapes my cousins

Pick till dusk, on the terraced slopes of Pelops.
Loaded vats of liquefaction. Lurid
Glow from deep in the valley steeped in blood feud.
And Demos still up to his churning thighs in purple.

TANTALUS

Sometimes the bright, incipient ripeness of what
I take to be a poem appears so close

It's as if my mouth were watering for the words
Whose urgent burgeoning it can almost taste.

But the greater the need to get it down in language,
The harder it is to write—which only makes more

Intensely visceral the need for the poem
To form the shape that culminates in speech.

And it's this thirsting, linguistic thing that vexes
Me so much it arouses a consummate

Desire for bodies I can't have: someone
I saw in the street, or someone from my youth.

Desire for words exacerbating the need
To be released from the need to express desire:

Solipsistic synergies of sex and syntax
Arrested by silence. A silence whose pressing, resistant

Insistence my mouth keeps straining against, contorted
By the arid ecstasies of self-estrangement.

Precipitous injunctions. Palpable absence.
That juicy, dangling, seedless pomegranate.

SPEECH CLASS

In grammar school, I couldn't pronounce my English.
At least not correctly enough. So twice a week
I was sent downstairs to practice *Enunciation*.
In concrete basement stalls where the dumb kids went.

Each time I spoke, my mouth was watched like a hawk.
I sweated reams when it came to phonemes and morphemes,
Flummoxed by possessives and silent vowels.
No end to the tongue-tied knots of a diphthong's tethers.

When Mrs. Segal, whose name I always botched,
Likened my spittle-lisp to a grazing cow
Chewing its cud, the placid, piebald boilers
Spat and hissed. The sibilance stuck in my teeth.

But walking home from school along Shore Drive,
Thálassa spoke to me in my parents' tongue,
The syllables as palpable as pebbles—
And me, by the waves, its fluent Demosthenes.

But I really wasn't at home in that language, either.
Betwixt and between, I stopped at the frothing lip
Of switchback currents. On protean Winthrop Beach.
When the sky turned overcast, and the whole Atlantic

Went dark as a blackboard chalked by the scavenger's shriek.
Then cloudy water, my favorite teacher. The old
Shape-shifter: "Repeat after me: *I'm nobody,*
But I can become whatever you want me to be."

Of course it was just the jetties, but when high waves
Were breaking over their arched and barnacled backs
My heart leapt up on cue, as if to a school
Of synchronized dolphins. *Delfinia,* trailing all kinds

Of impedimenta—the terms for which I lacked,
Beyond the usual almost phosphorescent
Glow of lolloping seaweed and clumps of kelp,
As vivid to me as vivisected meat.

Bladderwrack from blown-up Europe? On Winthrop
Beach the dolphins arrived without Arion,
But dragging what looked like his bloody singing robes.
Or a laundry load of my father's butcher's aprons.

If I can catch that shrill, re-circling cry
At just the right spontaneous pitch, I'm back
In Third Grade, hearing the prepubescent screech
Of laughter I caused by saying: *I was in Speech Class*

With Mrs. Sea Gull. Whose name was really *Segal*—
But not what I said when stern Miss Radcliffe asked me
To state the reason for my tardiness.
It was Poetry that made me late, for my life—

And here's my note, Miss Radcliffe. Mark it down
As wingéd words, but only if the lift
And let-down is one fell swoop of updraft. Then redraft.
Enunciation lessons with Mrs. Sea Gull.

ISLANDS

They're still going down in Seferis,
those boys who rock the boat
by pushing off with their feet

as corkscrews of foam unfurl
from the wake of their plunge, naked
bodies that blend with the blackness

that gleams on their skin from below,
which is where they go, down a passage
of language they swim through like water,

alive as they are to its every
shimmering waver, so young
they break the surface calm

with a coin between their teeth,
and leave those wide undulations
that shake the skiffs above them,

whose sails are ripped by the wind
and stitched by the sun's gold needles,
whose wooden keels, as they pitch,

are caulked with foam: he wrote it
down, in the turbulent-jubilant
wake of World War Two,

one morning when iridescent
the islands appeared, and the lush
Aegean as green as it ever

was in Aeschylus,
as green as that day when the bay
is *flowering with corpses,*

just as the herald tells us
it was, returning from Troy—
or was it from Salamis?

They're still going down in Seferis,
obliquely angling down
in the luminous gloom that keeps them

immersed in their element,
those naked divers holding
their breath as long as the breath

of the poem impels them to rhythmical
depths they couldn't have known,
converging on pebbles that lie

at the sandy bottom—and up
from which each body now smooth
as an ivory flask of oil.

DANDELIONS

Horta. A weed. But also their low-key way
Of exhorting how lucky we were. At those gatherings
When the tables were laden but the feast off limits,
Until they told us again about the "greens

Of the dandelion." And how salty they were when boiled
In the soot-black cauldrons of their turbulent epoch.
Those slender swaying tendrils, just fortifying
Enough to keep whole families alive.

Horta. Glottal clump with the pull of its
Uprootedness tenaciously intact.
Sinewy handfuls scavenged on scrawny goat-paths.
And we the seedlings of elders scattered like puffballs.

They sprang up again today, green stalks like the ones
In our own backyard, as I watched the harrowing news
From Sappho's golden island. Those dandelions
In an open field adrift with Syrians.

PHOTOGRAPH ALBUMS

"We finally got all of our family photos
Onto our home computer," Quentin was saying,
Just as we entered the Asian fusion place.

And that's when it hit me: all those leather albums
With their matted pages, gilt spines, and bristly hides,
In their mundane way as richly ceremonial

As the Golden Dragon preening its scales against
The restaurant window. All those cumbersome tomes,
In a decade or so defunct as the dinosaur.

But once the originals have been scanned and filed,
Why should it matter? By then the precious snapshots
Will have all gone into the world of light—

Or at least into cyberspace. Ancestral faces
That once unfurled from trays of salty water
As dark as Lethe, and then were pinned on strings,

Ex-voto like, and left to dry, will seem
A little less spooky-stern without the shades
Of their twentieth-century negatives to haunt us.

And pantheons of illumination so vast
They promised we'd see ourselves reflected in
Their image forever—*Olympus, Polaroid, Kodak*—

Will shrink to the candle-watt stature of Roman *Penátes*:
Household gods of birthdays and graduations,
Preservers of pointed hats and obnoxious horns.

Yet no chance then for an introverted child
To rummage inside a perfumed rosewood drawer
Until he comes across those jet-black volumes

As neatly stacked as the folded sweaters. Then home
Alone, and as the velvet pages open
To crinkly photos like pressed flowers, that boy

Might spend a whole afternoon just leafing through
The bulk of the family gatherings. I stare.
And there they are, and he, in plastic pockets.

Or fastened by all four corners. Or spilling out
Like a deck of cards that begs to be reshuffled.
An era no better or worse than now, but surely

The last to be cherished by a priceless, commonplace
Book designed for the usual, special occasions:
Christenings, weddings, bar mitzvahs, and senior proms.

But also vacations in Rambler station wagons,
And backyard cookouts. Goofy mug shots, cropped
Haphazardly as any selfie mélange.

Arcane compendiums, thick as The Yellow Pages.
And, because you have to hold them in your hands,
Heavy as the Tibetan Book of the Dead.

MY PHOTOGRAPH AT FIVE

Those thick black strands that snag in the plastic teeth.
My chin cupped in her hand, the searching gaze.

With my scalp still wet my mother has combed to one side
A perfect part in the waves. (But first straight down.

Dark curtain her art pulled almost over my eyes,
And only then drew back from the narrow seam

Dividing me from the older version of me
She lost at birth but seemed to see in my hair.)

And now I'm ready. I'm wearing my favorite shirt.
Navy blue with a light-gray collar. A jersey with sleeves

That cling as they stretch. (Its static gives it its shimmer.)
I like to keep this shirt buttoned up to my neck.

(My father, who doesn't speak much English, insists
On wearing an elegant tie with his butcher's apron.)

If my eyes look eager, the smile is melancholy.
Our album is filled with black-and-white shots of peasants.

Whoever I am I know I'm already in it.

II

SATURDAY NIGHT IN THE VILLAGE

Leopardi

As soon as the sun has set, that young woman
    Returning from the fields, the one who goes
To the festival every Sunday, has already picked
    The handful of flowers she'll wear tomorrow,
And carries them home with a bundle of kindling. Now
    That the day is over she has the violets
She needs to arrange her hair, and the roses to match
    Her dress, the dress that she'll wear tomorrow.

Sitting on the steps of her house, the old woman
    Facing the dusk picks up a thread
Of her neighbor's conversation and turns all their talk
    About tomorrow to the way it was
In her day, and the dresses she wore, and all the men
    That were mad about her; the old woman
Spinning her yarns about how light she was
    On her feet, her face radiant at dusk.

Already the darkness is filling the air we breathe;
    Already the sky is no longer azure;
Evening shadows now the slopes of the hills;
    Now the young moon is just beginning
To turn the rooftops white, as if the houses
    Were marked with chalk; and now and again
The mouth of a clanging bell is telling us something
    We already know: tomorrow is Sunday.

Still, when church bells ring the heart can't help
    Feeling a lift as the little children
Swarm the little piazza, shouting on the run
    As if they were heralds of leaping joy.
And even the farmer whistling to himself
    As the bells chime with the end of his day

In the fields, couldn't look any happier, relishing what's left
      Of those scraps he'll call supper when he gets home.

Sunday, the day of rest, cannot come fast
      Enough for the laborer, though it'll be over
Before he knows it. And now the lights of the houses
      Have all gone out, and the whole village
Is in the dark, not a murmur out of anyone—
      Except for the rasping sound of a saw
That works as they sleep, or the hammer blow that wakes
      The startled heart to its own pounding.

Which means the carpenter cannot yet afford
      To call it a day unless he has finished
One more job, polishing the grain of the wood
      Until it gleams without a trace
Of the sweat and blood it cost him; and dreading the light
      That shines through the cracks when Sunday dawns
On his shuttered windows, just as the dimming lantern
      Tells him it's time to close up shop.

Seven days of the week and only one
      That everyone always looks forward to
With a genuine sigh of relief. But when Sunday
      Finally arrives the mind is already
Drained by the usual concerns of the coming week,
      As if weariness and worry were the only
Outcomes we can always count on. Seven days,
      And this happiness that never stays

Longer than the little while it spends with us
      On Saturday evening . . . Little boy
So full of joy, so like this hour so like
      A flower whose blossom can bloom no further:
Do you know that the richest feast of your life is spread
      Before your eyes like clear blue skies

To an open bud? Enjoy it to the hilt,
      Because this is your moment of ultimate bliss.

About what happens next, I'd rather not say.
      But don't lose any sleep, my little friend,
Waiting for that festival they celebrate on Sunday.

BERLITZ SCHOOL OF LANGUAGE

"It's *vri-si,* not v*ri-shi,*" my teacher of modern Greek,
Who came from modern Greece, corrected me.
Her accent was subtle. Her English British. But her

Inflection of the demotic word for "fountain"
Lacked the shiny sibilant splash I always
Heard whenever one of the elders said *vrishí.*

Backwater speech that kept going back to its source—
Village springheads whose rustic mountain tongue
Still sang to us from the mouth of our kitchen faucet.

I was a graduate student taking a quick
Refresher course when I complained to my mother
About her pronunciation. Her people were Spartan.

She stood by the sink. "And where in Greece is she from,
This teacher of yours?" And when I say *Athens,* it's Athens
Dismissed with a wave of her laconic hand—

"Och . . . I knew it." And then again the sibilant
Gush of *vrishi* as fluent as faucet-water
Washing over the stack of stucco-white dishes.

ON THIS DAY I COMPLETE MY THIRTY-SIXTH YEAR

It's Independence Day. Our Greek-school teacher,
Mr. Nazariótis (we call him "Mr. Nazi"
Behind his back), points at the faded portrait
Above the map, and then at Missolonghi,
And tells us how *O Býronos* caught a fever,
And how the doctors had tried to save "The Poet."

Missolonghi, he says, is like Lynn Marsh,
Except with more mosquitoes. Leeches are worms
To suck the blood from the sick man's sweating back,
And drain the poison. Then he reads us some poems.
Forty years on, I hear Byron's ravishing English
Filtered through an accent so thick its nicotine rasp

Still rustles like sallow reeds in a shallow culvert.
Lord Byron's embroidered vest was ink-blotter velvet.
His tasseled fez was cocked at a jaunty angle.
His porcelain jaw as smooth as a jutting sink.
O warm, familiar blood the shades must drink
To speak in Hades; O immigrant voice that mangled

Magnificent verses, allowing me to hear them
In Greek broken English; O Poetry conjuring Freedom,
And the droning tenses of conjugated verbs;
O fever that feeds on the bold with a vampire's thirst,
And the jaundiced, unslakeable wit of the satirist;
O little church school between the sea and the suburbs!

JUST MY IMAGINATION

I was back in Winthrop, driving through the town
Where I grew up. The radio's off, but passing
By the brand new high school it's vintage Motown

Comes blaring through the Bose speakers in Neil
Shapiro's yellow Camaro. The top is down.
It's nineteen seventy-one. We're cruising the beach.

The great Temptations are singing as if they could drown
In the waves of what keeps running away with them.
I love the way they stretch out the crucial noun:

Imagin—a—shun. The girls on their towels are lying
Face-up or face-down. Their skin is golden-brown.
Neil is the president of the senior class

As well as the drama club. The sun is a crown
On his wavy luxuriant hair. Not one of our classmates
Is yet a shade in their underworld cap and gown

As Beauty walks by and he sings: *I hear a tender
Rhapsody, but in*—now slowing down—
Reality she doesn't even know me . . .

Then speeding up to flee her laughing frown.
But no fleeing *Myelofibrosis.* Mellifluous term
For the terminal cancer that never made a sound

As it pulsed to the tribal beat of his chosen blood.
And now there's no one around except the renown,
Smokey Robinson & the Miracles

Intoning their syrupy-scalding *Tears of a Clown*
They call *Pagli—a—chi.* Congenial Neil, as white
As a ghost as he waits for the vials to fill. The town

Conducting a blood-drive. The need for "Ashkenazi
Jews." The Mayo Clinic. The Music of Motown.
The reel-to-reel cassette not yet obsolete.

The canvas top on the yellow Camaro is down.
We're passing *The Neil Shapiro Center for
The Performing Arts.* He's Emerson College bound.

RECITING HENRY VAUGHAN IN THE MRI

He had no other way of getting through it.
So, flat on his back, yet prone to panic attack,
Cocooned as he was in that dark, cylindrical shaft,

He sang The Night to himself, his favorite poem:
"God's silent, searching flight . . . His still, soft call . . ."
Music he felt in the marrow of his bones,

Sore as they were from the aftereffects of chemo.
And as his stressed-out body was being scanned
By ultraviolet, cancer-detecting rays,

The vigilant meter kept trying its level best
To steady him, until he felt suffused
By the visionary poem's illumination:

"There is in God (some say) a deep, but dazzling
Darkness." And saying that, it leaves no doubt
Devotion's beautiful verse believes what it says

About salvation, alive as we are to the dead
Metaphysical poet's voice as it speaks to us
From out of the dark abyss he's singing about.

Inside the MRI the sick man recited
The Night, and truly however deep in his throat
The cancer was lodged, the song appeared to soothe

His rife-with-raging-cells esophagus.
Until the conveyor belt had carried him out
Of the concrete portal, out of the lyric poem's

Hermetic seal. And then, poor claustrophobic
Soul, he was back in the world of light—exposed
To the total, fluorescent, unfiltered, horror of

His final prognosis. And now not even tender
Henry Vaughan could help him get through the night.
And the *via negativa* was just that.

i.m. NN

ON THE SUFFERING OF THE WORLD

Schopenhauer opens the Upanishads.
Galaxies tremble, but not a living soul
To hear him gasp. Nothing to witness how

The great philosopher of Pessimism
Encounters the master text on Nothingness—
And nobody there to acknowledge it except

The knowledge that was there between those two,
Alone in a room that's neither here nor there,
East or West. Just Arthur Schopenhauer

Up all night, his countenance aglow
By a kerosene lamp: the human mind in total
Recognition of what it's reading, as if

An open book contained the darkness of being
Alone in the darkness. Enraptured as a spider
The Sanskrit articulates the web of the world

In page after page after page of infinite pain.
But the room is quiet as Bodhisattva's breathing,
The lamp a translucent globe of molten lava.

MEDICINE BALL

That brute dull thud of its lumpy leather pelt.
An exercise in oblivion's blunt obtuseness.

No wonder you turned around so I could see
How you rolled your eyes, still sharp enough to know

That this was dementia, and it was time to pass
The medicine ball around in a mindless circle,

Wheelchair by wheelchair. Around it comes again
In a waking dream—like the wrecking ball of a dream.

You rolled your eyes. And now the one who taught me
How to cradle a book in my hands, and read,

Holds out her hands to an object filled with sand.

RILKE REREADING HÖLDERLIN

Footnotes to the tower. For "He spends the summer
There, in a state of violent agitation,"
Read: "It's there, in his agitation's most violent
State, that Hölderlin suspends the summer"—
Like a yellow pear above the untroubled water.

For the lost, disheveled decades of derangement,
Translate *I was struck by Apollo* as you
Must change your life. For sonnets that sing their own
Spontaneous, Orphic necessity to praise,
Think naked as a lightning rod he waited.

For necessity insert *Ananke.* But for
Ananke, "Lord, just one more summer, please."
For summer, the lyre. Hölderlin in his tower.
Until autumn, when the leaves start falling. Whoever
Has nowhere to go will never get home now.

EPITHALAMIUM: THIRTY YEARS LATER

And gently now as with springtime clouds
May their heads be wreathed with marriage crowns.

   —Angelos Sikelianos

When, young, you stood together before the altar
And bowed your heads to what was over your heads
I was standing behind you, holding the orange blossoms.

Those crowns the *koumbáros* is called upon to crisscross,
Three times, *slowly,* above the bride and groom.
The right way to do it was right over left, but first

The softly fluttering petals must pass back over
Your heads the other way, and just as slowly,
Left over right. And always under the dark

Scrutiny of those front-pew elders, anxious
To see if I set the *stéfana* down correctly,
Right hand over left, the sign of flourishing luck.

(*Pure superstition,* yes, of course—but not,
At least with the flowers over your eyes, delusion.)
Now Dennis and Stephanie, young, look up from garlands

Woven from white silk flowers still trembling from my fingers.

MOON RIVER

Wider than a mile I'm crossing you in style
So Andy Williams would croon, when I was small

And my heart would lift to the tune that started with *moon*
Soaring like an open-voweled balloon

In the rising stress the singer gave to *river*
Whose gleam still streams in the rippling sheen of *wider*

And *mile* and me all ears a wide-eyed child
Of moonlit water's vast expanse as it flowed

From the living room and flooded our house with a sudden,
Melancholy kind of sheer elation—

As if I already knew that wide dark river
Was Lethe and nothing would ever cross back over

Its current in style but Music, moon-river music
My parents were listening to when Lawrence Welk

Was on and the shades were lamps in the living room.
All that came surging blindly back from the gloom

When I heard Ray Charles on NPR discuss
How he shucked the corny husks of the ancient chestnuts—

Except for the one by Andy Williams. "No way,
No how, can't touch Moon River," said Orphic Ray.

SWALLOW SONG

Not the Darkling Thrush, or Dickinson's "thing with feathers,"
Not Herbert's Easter Wings, or Shelley's Skylark,

Neither Hopkins in all his heraldic plumage,
Nor "Never Again Would Birds' Song Be the Same,"

And not that chelidon that flies to me
By way of the Waste Land, as if its Greek brought back

My long-departed parents' voices, singing
Their *chelidóni* songs to the cherished bird

Returning every spring to our back yard;
No, not even the Nightingale in Keats,

Or the Swans in Yeats, "mysterious, beautiful,"
But maybe more like the silent, wide-eyed look

Of the Parakeet trapped in Cornell's Box, tonight
It's those muffled, level tones of my poet-friend

Recalling his sick brave joke about lyric flight—
And how it was Tennyson's "O Swallow, Swallow"

That stuck in his throat as he sat beside the bed,
Watching the cancer choke his dying sister.

THE GOLDEN BOUGH

Maybe every poem is a Golden Bough
That leads to the poet's shades—or at least a lyric
Offshoot of its leafy original gleam.

Maybe every poem is a prayer to Venus,
Awaiting the sacred flutter that signals her doves
Alighting at the mouth of the Sibyl's cave.

Maybe every poem is the ancient passport
We need to embark with the sallow faces in steerage,
Seeking the father of the bloody family tree.

Maybe every poem is every poet
Returning through the Ivory Gate of Dreams,
Forgetting they ever drank from the jet-black river.

Maybe every poem is a Golden Bough—
Or at least a flicker from the tears of things.
Metallic shimmer of the continuous present.

IV

HADES

I was trying to hit, with a rock, a paper kite
My taunting cousin was flying above our yard—
But struck instead our black DeSoto's windshield.

And now my mother stands by the stove, arms
Akimbo but face beseeching him to go easy.
Just home from work, but still in his butcher's apron,

My father kneels before me. "Look me here."
I lift my head. Beholden to what his index
Finger won't let me avoid: those disappointed

Eyes of my immigrant father, who never struck me,
But whose old world admonitions always
Left me badly shaken—as if I'd betrayed

His grave injunction: *You my right hand.* But this time
He winks, and says instead: "Do you like Mamá
To make for you a baby sister, Yorgo?"

I think I nodded my head, then ran outside—
But not before I heard my mother's shriek
Of sheer elation's laughter. Sunlit and soaring.

Sometimes in dreams my father grips my shoulder.
"Look me here" he says, his glasses obscured
By smoky grease from the meats. Or the filth of Lethe.

And you, my right hand: so many errant throws,
But only one that cracks, with a rock, our black
DeSoto's windshield—and lets me hear their laughter.

My parents. Down there where nothing breaks the silence.

HALLUCINATION

Another haunting symptom her late Dementia
Won't let me forget. I mean that night I found her
Sitting straight up in bed. All glassy-eyed:

"Look at him. Oh look at how tired he is.
My father. He has to carry that heavy jar
Of olives and nobody on the trolley car

Will give up their seat for him. He's so so tired.
And he has to lug that big heavy jar in his arms,
Way up to the top of Johnny Cake Hill. And damn

Those Italians—they buy so many Kalamata
Olives from us. Is that all they ever eat?
Just look at him, poor thing. He's dead on his feet."

My mother, envisioning her immigrant father
At the foot of the bed, riding the trolleys.
Pallas Athena, gray-eyed goddess of olives.

LOVE

Apokatástasi. New Testament Greek
For a world completely restored—and where in the world

Is that, unless it's the faithful plentitudes
Of Shakespeare and Proust, the Delft of exacting Vermeer?

But yesterday that frisky Alaskan Husky
Was lifted up over the bars of the hospital bed,

And hunkered down upon the blanketed, upturned
Feet of Mrs. Aphrodite Darris.

"He's trained for this," the nurse in hospice whispered.
"He brings good energy . . ." That's when I heard

The most beautiful voice in the choir, silenced by cancer
But singing through her eyes: our Aphrodite

With all her children and grandchildren gathered around.
Everyone finding it hard to speak, yet laughing

Out loud at the dog so fervently wagging its tail,
Whose breed was from a place so cold it must

Know all about how to warm the feet about
To step down into the icy currents of Lethe,

But not yet ready to go. She patted his head.
Open wide were the crimson jaws of Orcus.

But here the panting dog was palpable joy.
But then again the *Apokatástasi*—

The world of catastrophic pain restored,
As the husky departs. Now she who was my brother's

Second mother closes her eyes, and doesn't
Open them up again until her ancient

Name is being called by Father Nick.
And then her anointed eyes are closed for good.

STELE

In the famous frieze of Orpheus and Eurydice,
The one at the national museum in Naples
 (Though once it was used to mark a young wife's grave),

Each lover, to Rilke, is touching the other so lightly,
Their trembling seems untouched by fear of parting.
Each lover so full, he says, of tenderness,

Possession plays no part in their desire,
Like figures about to merge in a ballroom mirror.
Oblivious love. Music that froze Oblivion.

Orpheus is holding his lyre. Which means that beyond
The frieze the writhing snakes in the Gorgon's hair
Have been put to sleep, or turned themselves to stone.

Orpheus is holding his lyre. A flock of notes
Still hangs in the air—the only birds in Avernus.
Released from his torturous wheel, as it ticks to a halt,

Ixíon thinks his luck has turned at last.
Now Sisyphus straightens up, like Leopardi's
Laborer, about to sing at the end of his day.

Still, here in the frieze, each pair of stone feet is moving
Its pivoting sandals in another direction,
As Hermes taps Eurydice on the shoulder,

Cutting in on the last dance of the night,
The dance the carving depicts in the Naples museum,
That stele once used to mark a young wife's grave.

THE HORSES OF ACHILLES

Cavafy

When the horses of Achilles turned and saw
Patroclus dead, that beautiful young man,
So brave and strong, they both began to weep.
Suddenly that Olympian breed felt bewildered
By death's outrageous display of what it is.
No matter how they arched their necks, and tossed
Their wild, luxuriant manes, or stamped their hooves
As if to wake him up, they couldn't shake off
What they were seeing, seeing it there in the dirt:
That heap of flesh and bones with the pitiful look
Of Patroclus. Their rider's breath was gone.
Now he was nothing—nothing now and nowhere.

But now it was Zeus who was moved, and seeing all
That was happening to that immortal pair,
He wondered why he'd been so foolish, once.
"Surely it would have been better, my dear sad horses,
If I had never offered you as a gift
At the wedding feast of Peleus and Thetis.
What on earth were the two of you doing down there,
Yoked to the cars of such pathetic creatures?
Mortals are nothing but the dust at your heels.
Old age and death can never catch up with a steed
That flies like the wind. And yet you carry on
As if men had bridled you to their misery."

But those two gallant horses kept right on weeping,
Weeping for Patroclus, still shedding their tears
As if there was no end to what they felt.

SPRING

But the breath of a man will not come back . . .
　　　　—Iliad, Book IX

The latticework of that garden gate
Next door, its latch so loosely bolted,

Or so lightly fastened, the slightest breeze
Can shake it, as though in agitation.

That garden gate like a stable door
The wind keeps softly butting against.

Then even the flower beds are still
As the dark night sky.
　　　　　　　　Achilles, again,

Reminding me that being alive
Is only the restlessness of the breath,

And once it escapes entirely, over
The *erkos,* the little fence of the teeth—

No one can hunt it back again.
And yet the poem, at a later time,

In a different mouth, may live in the breath.
But where has he gone? the horses lament,

Their flowing manes like the chestnut trees
Transfixed by the dirt. And then again

In the slightest breeze the ancient rejoinder:
Over the little fence of the teeth.

MIMNERMUS (7TH CENTURY BC)

When Sappho says: "He melts the limbs like wax,"
She's singing of Eros, who also immures in us
What happened then in uncongealing amber—
Which scalds us all the more as we remember
How adamant once, for us, was the god of sex.

"But would it be *life*, and what is *that*, when golden
Aphrodite is finally gone?" Mimnermus
Hoped to die before he could answer this question.
Cavafy describes arousing himself to write
By "invoking the shades." Alone, by candlelight.

OPEN CASKET

According to Pavese, *when Death arrives*
It'll have your eyes. And exactly what that unflinching
Quote implies, these sleeping lids would, if they could,
Disclose: nothing embalms the fervent gaze.

In Lampedusa's novel, the one it took him
A lifetime to write, the Leopard looks in a mirror,
And wonders aloud why no one's allowed to die
Unless they're wearing a face that's not their face.

And now those slender hands, precise as birds
Intent to cut the imperturbable air,
Are lying serenely folded over Peter's chest.
They make their point. My tender, sardonic friend,

Unable to stomach another empty suit
That's full of smarmy imposture, but spelling out
The auspices as best he can. One more
Passionate lesson in stark, Italian Realism.

i.m. PC

THE SOURCE OF THE STYX

From Pheneos, following Helios, it's only
A day's journey to reach the source of the Styx.
Stay left of the trees, beyond their beseeching shade,

Till Nonakis, the city where nothing exists,
Not even its ruins. Then, just as Kylléne's peak
Breaks up what's left of the light, it dawns on you:

Niagara Falls of Nightfall. Cataracts so
Opaque they could be six feet away, or else
Six hundred. And there you are, in Stygia,

Transfixed by its pitch-black pools. Dark ink of *Ananke*,
Where everything's already written. Looming cliffs
That comb the sheer flux of the current's flow like flax.

By you and your dead, great Styx, the radiant gods
Still swear their redundant oaths, your banks the brackish
Rebuke to all that solemn, Olympian rubbish;

Neck deep, down there, in the marshes, for nine long years
Is the price of their betrayal—the gods, like Oblivion's
Frogs, immersed in the oozing miasmas they caused.

Assiduous Styx, acid that nothing resists:
It eats through agate and glass, recalcitrant potsherds,
Horn and bone—even iron and bronze and lead.

To it all forms, at the core, are hollow forms.
From Pheneos, following Helios, it's only
A day's journey to reach the source of the Styx.

Stay left of the trees, beyond their beseeching shade,
Till Nonakis, the city where nothing exists,
Not even its ruins. Then, just as Kylléne's peak

Breaks up what's left of the light, it dawns on you:
Niagara Falls of Nightfall . . .

TONSILS

You got there early, and being a young mother
Eager to pick up her child and bring him home,
It caught you off guard—not knowing I'd been moved

From my private room. Nor did the overnight nurses
Tell me the sleepy kid they were wheeling in
To take my place was just my age, and had

Leukemia—although I couldn't help seeing
His shaven head. (O sallow lolling head!)
He caught you off guard. And put you in panic mode.

Until the corridors led to my crowded ward.
No wonder that morning my sliding plastic curtain
Went flying back on its hooks. And just like that

Oblivion's veil is rent, and there I am,
Back in your breathless-for-me, rock-solid embrace.
As if I could feel what the hero had failed to feel,

Although three times he tried to wrap his arms
Around the dear but unsubstantial shade.
Of course the flashback is gone in a nanosecond.

And just like that you're back down there—down there
With ancient Antikléia. And then again
That changeling boy the nurses keep wheeling in.

AT THE GRAVE

The sun was shining. The priest was chanting.
Each one of us was holding a rose.
The casket lay on brass supports.

But there was that space between the bars
Of the trestles, that crisscross space just low
Enough for a child to look down through . . .

The sun was shining. The priest was chanting.
Each one of us was holding a rose.
The casket lay on brass supports.

Although it was long before I heard
Of Blaise Pascal, there was that space
Between the bars. That space. That space . . .

HONEY

1

Meli. To Winthrop it comes like a melody
In a gallon jar. And ever so sweetly my cousin
Tells me: "I brought it for you, from Ákovos."

Unprocessed honey . . . straight from the village hives.
Before I'm able to process what that means,
My cousin Perry unscrews the airtight lid.

Meli. As in the mouth of an open jar
That lavishes the tongue with a dripping spoonful
Of amber-gold. As in the honeybees

That swarmed to Pindar's open mouth as he slept
In the shade of a sacred oak—sweet child who woke
To the odes of praise with *meli* on his lips.

My cousin was seven when he fell from a tree,
And broke his arm in two places. The village doctor
Botched the job, and, fearing infection, and lacking

The money to send him to Athens, his panicked parents
Called our house. As soon as my father hung up,
But still talking village Greek, he said to my mother:

"Let's bring the boy here, to the Boston hospitals."
"But how? He can't just hop on a plane. He has
To get through immigration, and that takes years."

"But you with your English can talk to the Senator.
Go to the State House. The Kennedys love the Greeks."
And there I am, at six years old, listening

To Ted Kennedy tell my mother how much
He loved to dine at Anthony's Pier Four.
And how he knows all the Greek waiters by name.

2

A month or so later, my cousin's right elbow is bent
As stiff as a board when he arrives at our house,
In Winthrop, along with his younger brother Peter.

Light-years later, as if it was all immured
In *meli,* my cousin Pericles holds out
A jar of amber-gold in his supple arms.

His kids have kids. He's sixty-six, and ready
To hang up his wings as an Air Canada pilot.
Airtight the past congeals and uncongeals.

Heals and unheals. But Peter is always thirty.
What tastes like viscous honey? *Younger the brother.*
What feels like vicious migraines? *Malignant the tumor.*

O helpless village parents, whose peasant spells
Can ward off the Evil Eye but not the petrified
Look in the pleading eyes of your dying son

As he lay in Intensive Care—hooked up to glowing
Screens in the vast complex of humming cells
At the Mass General in downtown Boston.

Brute mortality. Sweet, enigmatic *meli.*
As in melancholic Lucretius coating the lip
Of the metaphorical cup with lyric honey,

To make his bitter medicine palatable—
Distilled as it was from vintage Stoic wormwood.
How many cells of how many honeycombs

Does it take to fill a gallon jar of *meli?*
Enough for the hives to glow in two places. As if
The honeybees of Ákovos had flown

To Wínthropos. The Kennedys love the Greeks.

V

PROTEUS IN WINTHROP

I'm squeezing his hand, but he speaks another tongue.
The word for his walking stick, like the hiss of the surf

At our feet, is an eel so quick it could slither away
With a single wriggle: *gklítsa*. The breakers don't move

But the pebbles keep shifting places. If I had to guess,
He must be as old as old Proteus himself.

Very soon, I'm told, he'll be going back to Greece.
By now we've reached Seal Harbor, the end of the beach.

I don't yet know the names of the harbor islands
But I think I know the myths. And the fog is lifting.

I point to the islands and say the only thing
I ever remember saying to him: *Elláda*.

His name for home. He nods to me by the waves.
In a week or so he's gone. And then he's the waves.

LVOV

To go to Lvov . . . when the suitcases gleam with dew . . .
As they always do, each time I read the opening
Lines of Adam Zagajewski's great poem.

And then again near the end, when he says Lvov
Is everywhere and everyone is a Jew—
At least in the moment of leaving their home behind.

So too there was dew on those ancient steamer trunks
Still held together with rope, too big and unwieldy
To angle cleanly through our back porch door.

Lugubrious old-world luggage. Brass hasps and clasps.
Scuffed-up third-class freight whose velvet lining
For all I knew went back to the Ottoman Empire.

Strangers that seemed to show up out of nowhere,
At least to us kids. And sometimes late at night,
When all the kitchen commotion woke us up.

Small chips of paint, scraped off the jambs of the door.
Relatives I didn't know from Adam—
But there they are, in Zagajewski's poem,

Where everyone comes with some kind of baggage. As if
Those low unsettling voices that came from our kitchen
Would ever be able to tell me how heavy it was.

CALCHAS READING THE SIGNS

Whatever he saw, whatever he felt or smelt
In that smoky dripping handful of purple entrails
Just thawing out from the freezer, the news from Athens
Was ominous, and he wouldn't haruspicate
On how and when the Colonels might react—
But the gobbets of offal keep piling up in the pail.

It's not that he fully trusted the lordly voice
Of the BBC, but hearing *Vietnam*
He drops what he's doing, and cranking up the volume
On that crackly little Panasonic—
That's when I hear it too: *Khe Sanh.* It's what
Comes through the speaker's throbbing bamboo mesh

As I'm stamping prices on jars of baby food:
A staticky hiss like burning jungle grass . . .
My father wiping his hands on his butcher's apron,
Oblivious to his customers as he listens
To a transistor radio broadcast the blood
Of a world in shambles. And then he's back at his block.

Khe Sanh. My older cousins, George and Jimmy,
Are loading up the van they'll drive around Winthrop,
Delivering groceries and checking out girls.
I'm stamping the Gerber's jars of baby food.
Nobody knows whose number will come up.
But our Calchas isn't taking any chances.

Already he's built another hecatomb,
And now he's scrutinizing some gristly turkey
Intestines unfurling for all I know like the coils
Of giant lianas he saw in Guadalcanal
As a young recruit. But through that throbbing bamboo
Mesh I hear the Hydra's serpentine hiss

He heard as a village boy way up in the Peloponnese.

ASTORIA

That's Whitman in Greek town, before there were enough
To call it *Greek town,* or so I imagine, reading

His poem, "Proud Music of the Storm," and stopping,
Electrified by the lines: *Again, at Eleúsis,*

Home of Ceres, I see the modern Greeks dancing,
I hear them clapping their hands as they bend their bodies,

I hear the metrical shuffling of their feet
In some louche dive taverna, and Whitman dancing

With the men, at least in the turning lines, which move
To the clapping hands of their own impromptu beat,

The bodies bending, lank as the wheatfields of Ceres.
I picture dark *pallikária* ("youngbloods" they call them),

Dancing there for themselves, and drinking with Whitman,
After the Civil War. Their country's freedom

Is young as they are, young as demotic song.
Young as the aftermath of ancient blood feud,

When upstart Liberty sings of starting anew.
And then *again,* at *Eleúsis, home of Ceres,*

And in Astoria too, the muffled procession
And secret initiation rites of tribal

Purification, still impure as ever.
I hear them clapping their hands as they bend their bodies,

I hear the metrical shuffling of their feet
In some basement taverna, with sawdust strewn on the floor.

Like the one in Lowell my father took me into
When I was a boy, and dropped off his father there,

One listless Sunday. The old men playing cards
At a smoky table. The smoky glasses of ouzo.

The faintly screeching pitch of a clarinet solo.
And two men dancing slow, in a dark corner.

Proud Music of the Storm, I found it in *Autumn
Rivulets,* I felt it in flowing bloodlines:

My Homer of *Drum-Taps,* Cavafy of *Calamus* reeds.

THE FUNERAL ORATION, 431 BC

The wagons are loaded down with their draped caskets.
The widows are holding back their lamentations.
The horses' hooves are restless in their restraints.

By the Tomb of the Unknown Soldier, the speaker stands
On a raised platform. But it's thanks to Thucydides
His voice will carry down through the centuries.

The Peloponnesian War has just begun,
Yet Pericles in his speech has already proved
Demokratía immortal—at least in the future

Perfect of Attic Greek at its glorious height.
Imperial Pallas Athena, her helmet uplifted,
Listens intently. There's nothing under the sun

As new as the Parthenon in its virginal marble.
Banished now the blind bard from the Polis.
Aesthetic Athens replaces Tragic Troy.

The City of Logos, whose gates are always open
To foreigners, especially those with nothing
To declare but their undeniable genius,

Is also the City of Eros, whose citizen-body
Will fight for their beloved like an *erastés*—
A fiercely devoted, aggressive lover. The Spartans,

Of course, are formidable opponents. Consider
Their iron discipline, the honor-bound
Advance of their phalanx, and try not to flinch. But tribal

Insulation, combined with suspicion of open
Spaces designed for debate—a sunlit agora
Or Boston Common—will doom their way of life.

And now the most resounding lines of all:
"What we have achieved, my dear Athenians,
Will be an education for the world."

(Aglitter with dew is the grass at Gettysburg.)
And then, at the turn of a page: incurable plague.
Affliction, whose powers of articulation

Not even Athens can fathom, yet symptom by symptom
The spasms recorded in dense, Hippocratic detail.
And then again in dense, photographic detail.

Lucid the shrouded lens of Mathew Brady.
Grainy the film that crops the sprawling fields.
Turn the page and it's Whitman dressing the wounds.

"Impromptu" the hospital-church. Unspeakable
The lack of anesthetic. Torch-lit the tender,
Surgical helplessness of lyric precision.

And time and again as the ancient entropic cycle
Devolves, turning the Demos to Demogorgon,
Those massacres at Melos and My Lai.

But first that section on Corcýra's altars,
Murderously stained with the filial blood
Of the murderous suppliants that clung to them.

That primal section like a vivisection
Of Propaganda spawning Fanaticism
And all that flows in its wake, as honest speech

And common decency dissolve—and all
So purely distilled by all those verses beginning
With "and" in Shakespeare's sonnet sixty-six:

And needy nothing trimm'd in jollity,
And purest faith unhappily forsworn,
And guilded honor shamefully misplaced,
And maiden virtue rudely strumpeted,
And right perfection wrongfully disgraced,
And strength by limping sway disabléd,
And folly (doctor-like) controlling skill,
And simple truth miscall'd simplicity,
And captive good attending captain ill.

But *art made tongue-tied by authority?*
Not when the audience clamors for Pasternak
To read "the sixty-six" in their native Russian.

But first it's turncoat Alcibiades
In Spartan tunic, shorn of his flowing, luxuriant
Hair but not of his charismatic genius.

Enter Syracuse. The fleet destroyed.
The marble quarries packed with Athenians—
As if the whole endeavor were one big theater

Of Dionysus. *Total Annihilation,*
Thucydides called it, quoting Herodotus
Accounting for Persian losses at Salamis.

The term redundant. The irony consummate. "Perish,
Enlightened by the vollied glare," writes Melville,
As the march into Virginia ends in the First

Manassas. And then again in Thomas Hobbes,
Translating *The Peloponnesian War* as training
For *Leviathan,* the work he pledged

To the Commonweal, and to his dear companion,
Sidney Godolphin, that "most worthy brother . . .
Unfortunately slain . . . in the Publique quarrel,

By an undiscerned and an undiscerning hand."
And *then* by implacable *then—O Captain! My Captain!—*
Set down in the grave, unfinished, exacting prose

Of the exiled general, Thucydides,
Lamenting his dearly beloved Pericles—
Forever lost to the Plague. And lost to the Polis.

MIDNIGHT MASS

Even before the Easter candles were lit,
Illuminating the grainy lines of their faces
There in the darkened church, I knew how tired

And weighted down those immigrant laborers were,
And just by hearing the creak of their crowded pews.
At stroke of midnight, when everyone rose to sing

Christós Anésti, and I could believe my ears.
As if the wood had sounded the timbre of sheer
Exhaustion's faith, and I felt it in my bones.

All the aches and pains in that lurching yet limber way
The congregation got to its restless feet.
En masse, but not in blind obedience.

Not even the groaning wood in Grünewald—
As under the weight of the Word the beam of the cross
Contracts—uplifts me now like that supple creak

I heard at stroke of midnight. When everyone rose,
At least to sing in the dark. Including those front-pew
Elders, standing without their canes and their walkers.

RCA VICTOR

It's the O in Victrola, as dark as the O
In Gladiola is golden, opens
The mouth of my uncle's shade, who tells me
About the abyss in the ancient brass horn

Of a record player. The one he sent
To his mother in Ákovos, way up
In the Peloponnesos, whose songs
Are steeped in open vowels, whose echoes

I hear in *pólemos*: my father's
Brother's word for war, whose O's
Go back to Homer, whose gift was the brute,
Operatic, music of *pólemos*.

It's the O at the end of *Figaro*
(Or a figment of my imagination)
Allows me to overhear those full-throated
Officers singing, as Mozart blares

From the confiscated Victor-Victrola.
But it's only when my uncle pronounces
Phonógraphos the antique crankshaft
Revolves in my hand, and sets the valley

Echoing with all those O's—
A disk so dark not even some golden
Silver Age arpeggios
Could lighten the shade of the olive groves.

It's a month before the plastic O
Of the breathing tube was put in his mouth
My uncle tells me about the bonfire—
Just so that I know how the village glowed.

It's Germans burning the furniture,
And some of the houses, before they go.
It's the muted O in *gramophone*
And my grandmother's obdurate ghost, who won't

Let go of the brazen O of its horn;
It's the screech of the swallowed O in *Phoenix,*
And the O in the middle of *immolation*—
That smoldering unmollified O.

And now it's the O at the end of *Velcro*
That straps the tube to his open mouth,
And keeps the dying fable ablaze
In my uncle's throat unspeakable.

It's my aunt from Ákovos, the only
One alive who would know, saying "*Oxi*—
Nazis no kill her. I hear she die
Of stroke . . . But me too young to know."

It's those rows of Oleanders leaning
Partisan this way, collaborant that—
Depending upon who swung from them—
My cousin Angélo must pass below

To get to our *yiayia's* overgrown stone:
The one Oblivion's river, however
The Oleanders hover over
The names, flows under just the same.

It's the O in the Ouzo that Angie pours,
And showing us her photos, *lo,*
Of a date engraved in granite. A date
That's later than the close of the war.

Yet does it denote the year of death,
Or the atonement of re-interment,
Dear cousin? We toast your devotion, but drink
Oblivion's river, smoky as Ouzo.

Smoky as the ossified O
Of the open pit where the bones are exhumed.
O record revolving on Clotho's spindle,
Verse-needle at home in the line's dark groove—

O flaming, familial, apocryphal
Tongues: the O in Victrola dark
As the O in Gladiola is golden
Mozart. Sing, by osmosis, O Muse.

PAUSANIAS (2ND CENTURY AD)

For twenty years, as long as the hero took
To get to Troy and back to Ithaka,

I walked and walked the whole of conquered Hellas,
My odyssey without the archipelagoes,

But plenty of hybrid monsters of local legends.
Methodical as a snail, I was the one

The Arcadians trusted to view the fabled oar
The wanderer must carry across his shoulders

As if he was yoked to it—until, as the prophet
Instructs, he gets to a place in the Peloponnese

Where the only waves those people know are wheat.
Up there, by the windswept marble threshing floors,

I saw the sky-dipped blade of the great endeavor
Still trailing moss of wild Poseidon's beard.

And just as the prophet Teiresias once predicted,
The wanderer's oar was called a *winnowing fan.*

I set it down in my guide to the sacred sites
For Roman tourists. And then I walked back home.

MYCENAE REVISITED

He kept going back to the phrase, "inside the wall,"
Convinced that a cryptic passage in Pausanias
Led to the beehive tombs, preserved in amber—

If Heinrich Schliemann understood the grammar.
Glory congealed. Kleos bright as the disk
Of the sun god, Ra. The mask of Agamemnon . . .

And was it a fluke, or an omen, the text came roughly
Seventeen-hundred years after the fall of Troy,
And here he was, consulting it as his guide,

Seventeen-hundred years later? From gaps in the text
He tapped dark sleep for the glint of gilded dream-vessels,
Heard loose millennial sediment sifted through shovels

Sunk into vast and vaguely oracular lacunae.

2

An hour from Argos, my Uncle Taki's cellar.
Or bunker. Damp clay floors and hurricane lamp.
The gleam of purple grapes in open bins,

Their juice transfused through coils of plastic tubes.
Ensconced on crates, we toasted the *kefalotíri:*
Those thick rank heads of cheese suspended by strings,

Their goat's milk cured by hanging from the rafters.
My uncle called them *The Colonels* . . . Porous and moist
The breathing earthen walls of the Peloponnese.

As redolent as ever that village cheese
In the aftermath of the junta. As pale as ghosts
Those homemade heads still floating in the dark

Of Uncle Taki's cellar. Or bunker. An hour from Argos.

3

Trenches cut at the close of the nineteenth century.
Scaffolds propped at steep angles. The site gouged out.
Inside the wall. Go back to an earlier entry.

Read it again. Bear down on the relevant terms.
Inside the word for *wall* the sound of *fate.*
Teixei implied in *teixoi.* Burial chambers

As echo chambers. Pore over *periboli,*
The circular border enclosing a sanctuary.
Under a sandy hill, parabolic passages.

The convoluted plots and unsettled ashes
Turning over like syntax in an hour glass.
Inside the wall. Beneath the earth. That burnished

Threshold where staunch Orestes unsheathed his hesitant blade.

4

In the famous photograph of Schliemann's Greek bride,
She's wearing the jeweled headdress, necklace, and earrings:
Adornments from Troy: Sophia at Seventeen.

THE OLD COUNTRY

Convenient, catch-all lingo. Allowing my father
    To tell us where he was coming from
        Without going into all
            The murky details.

Though just the same a shadowy flicker of fear
    And humiliation, perhaps even pent-up
        Rage, seemed to play over
            His open face—

Before those deflected feelings went veering off,
    Like a school of minnows just under the surface
        Wince that came with his phrase:
            The old country.

That wary, throwback expression that kept his past
    At bay, even as it reminded him
        Those days were only a tribal
            Stone's throw away.

A term he tossed off without shrugging it off, yet casting
    The tender net of his reticence wide
        Enough for a calm expanse
            To settle around us.

It was a wintry gust off the wild Atlantic,
    And summer curtains billowing open
        As sunlight comes darting through
            A rusty screen.

As if the century's blood-red interstices
    Were trawling in time still over our heads,
        Like a dappled mesh we'd always
            Be small enough

To slip through unscathed, and just by keeping things vague.

MAVRO DAPHNE

If Rilke once pressed his hand to the trunk of a laurel,
Then drew it back, claiming he felt a heart
Throbbing inside that column of writhing bark,

And sunlit Apollo, still there in pursuit, as well,
It was squat gallon jars on our cellar floor, kept cool
By the damp concrete, and filled with dark red wine,

Sent a strange chill through me as I came to grips
With what I was sent to fetch. And always more
Still waiting to pour from the cask, whose copper spigot

Kept it in check and doesn't let me forget
That bulging, boding oak barrel. Just biding its time.
Connected by dripping coils to our homemade still.

Mavro Daphne. It sloshed against my chest
When I carried a jar upstairs, as if its Greek
Concoction was ready to burst from the airtight cork

That was stuck in its throat. But slow secretions came first.
Impressions formed by an iron clamp, and the ooze
That flowed through plastic tubes from purple grapes:

As if the bitter essence of certain ominous
Things—like the fate of Aunt Pota's older brother,
Shot in the head at the end of the civil war—

Was being instilled without my being told.
But it won't mature till those indelible Rorschach
Blots on the basement floor keep spreading further,

Becoming my own, as they darken, flesh and blood.

VI

ONE-CREDIT SEMINAR ON THE ODES OF HORACE

We were sitting around a polished oak table, just getting to
    Those famous lines near the end of the Sestius Ode:
Revenant whitefaced Death is walking not knowing whether
    He's going to knock at a rich man's door or a poor man's
When one of the students (Andrew) said it was "totally weird"—
    Which led us to look at the paleness of Death's appearance,
Whose pallor is what, when he comes, comes with him: the sickness
and shock
    In his ghastly face. And that's where we stopped. And then
It was Jennifer's email, saying: "I'm sorry for missing class,
    But I'm having panic attacks. I keep flashing back
To March 19th, when I entered my dorm room and found my boyfriend
    Dead of an overdose . . . I can get you a note . . .
What reading should I do to be prepared for next week?"

O goodlooking fortunate Sestius, don't put your hope in the future;
    The night is falling; the shades are gathering around;
The walls of Pluto's shadowy house are closing you in.
    There who will be lord of the feast? What will it matter,
What will it matter there, whether you fell in love
    With Lycidas, this or that girl with him, or he
With her? So David Ferry's rendering goes, its tone
    Of tender, knowing, bemusement faithful to Horace's
Pitying voice, but whose pity has come to speak to us
    Through the whitefaced mouth of revenant Death, still going
From house to house, until he gets to Jennifer's dorm room.

And what will it matter now if Andrew was drawn to the line
    About fishermen *hauling their caulked boats down to the water?*
It's late September. We're sitting around a polished oak table
    Whose wood is sacred to Jove, whose lightning bolt
Has already sounded deep in the heart of Indian summer.

93

Last night our oldest friend turned Oedipus at
Colonus. It happened right after his shaky great reading.

He stood unfolding his orthopedic cane
Atop the steps behind the Poetry Center,

His macular degeneration now having
Advanced so far he seemed oblivious

To all but the darkness his feet were about to enter.
And waving off our annoying flurry of hands

With his patient-impatient: "Go on ahead. Go on!"
We watched from the lamp-lit curb as he tap-tap-tapped

Each granite step. Tap-tap-tapped as if
Instructing us on how he kept his meter.

Call it blindly descending, Sophoclean
Ferocity of focus before an abyss,

But also the delicate steps of our elderly friend—
Still trusting the tremulous earth he walked on, but not

Expecting the Door of Love to suddenly open
(As it does for Oedipus in the denouement).

His heart was in his hand, and his hand was holding
His folding cane like a shepherd's willowy wand.

FIRST STEPS

My brother was three years old when he got to his feet
And finally started to walk on his own. And if
I was older than him by just enough to remember
How it happened, it's only because the snow
Was falling softly in our picture window.
Fifty years must pass before I really
Hear the urgency in my grandfather's Greek
As he whispers to my mother: "No! Don't touch him."

The heat is coming through the metal bars
Of the radiator that's warm to my brother's tiny,
Epic grip as he struggles to pull himself up.
He takes two steps. Then looks around, and plops
Back down on the parlor carpet. My mouth is open—
But the snowflakes are silent as they melt on my tongue.

RESURRECTION

Alanus ab Insulis insisted the soul
Gets fastened to the body "with tiny little nails."
With tiny little medieval nails

The Latin term for their fineness—*subtilibus*—
Attaches itself to my childhood memory,
And won't let go. As if our Byzantine Christ,

Cocooned in a golden nimbus, had floated up
Again from the Cross, like a butterfly of light.
And just those three little pinpricks of his blood,

Before there was ever any rent in my belief.

HOLY FRIDAY

In the middle of the afternoon. When only
Mothers and children were lined up at the altar,
Waiting to go under the *Epitáphios.*

Christ's tomb. A canopy of open blossoms
Over a wooden table. The snow-white tablecloth
Sprinkled with pink rose petals. A pair of candles.

Here you crossed yourself and kissed the icon
Of the Savior's sleeping face, whose lacerated
Brow and cheeks were smeared with traces of lipstick.

Then it was down on all fours, as one by one
We entered the sacred by crawling under a table
No bigger than the one in our kitchen. On Holy

Friday, flush with that lush, red velvet carpet
That runs along the nave—your one and only
Lasting intimation of another life:

Mother and child, come up on the other side.

WALK-IN FREEZER

Not as big as the vault in the bank, whose shiny door
The teller unlocks with a special key, but heavy
Enough that its iron handle was child resistant.

Nothing gave me the shivers like seeing my father
Backing out of its icy blast with a shank
Of lamb on his shoulder, his face gone white as a sheet

As he turns from the groaning hinges and drops the meat
On his block. Before I ever heard the word
For it was *carcass,* it made a sickening thud.

So many times I saw him go into the freezer
At closing time, yet I was taken aback
Each time that foot-thick door slammed bolted shut

Behind my father, and made the sawdust jump,
And shook the blades, up there, on their overhead rack.
Not even Damocles' sword could make me feel

The pendulous precariousness of it all
Like looking up agog at all those dangling
Cleavers and knives and saws. In their *clink* and *glint*

I hear my listening left to its own devices—
Suspended till now. Too late the latent Muse
Of anticipation sharpens her instrument.

Too soon those Saturdays meant we were closed, and I
Was done with scooping the damp handfuls of sawdust
Out of a burlap sack and going backwards

Down the vacant grocery aisles, eager
To walk back home with my father. A suppertime walk
That was mostly in silence, when silence was golden—just

As the song would have me believe. If only as golden
As those sallow flakes I flung across the floor,
As if I was sowing the faded hardwood with seeds.

And after the sawdust it's that tree-lined sidewalk,
As quiet as every muffled step we took
In the scattered light of dusk, our time together . . .

Fluorescent, closing-time hum of the empty store.
Some shards of melting ice on his chopping block
Have darkened the grain of the wood. The sawdust is down.

I'm waiting for my father, who's still inside the freezer.

MY GUIDES

However heavy their winter overcoats
And muddy their clodhopper shoes, not even Hermes

Can pass between worlds as swiftly as they can, and do—
When I recall their halting, broken speech.

They tell me about Poseidon, how wild he was
On their transatlantic crossings. Although their knowledge

Of the Inferno doesn't extend to the deepest
Rings of the Twentieth Century, what they saw

Is dark enough for their cigarettes to glow
Like the fireflies in Dante. My guides. They come

Whenever they're summoned, but our conversations
Always end at the same impasse: they ask

Me why I never married, and don't have children.
They fear my DNA to wander, in exile.

They tell me I wasn't made to weave my own shroud.
My old-school uncles scrutinize me like tailors

Threading the eye of a needle—and then they're gone,
Swifter than Hermes with his magic wand.

HORACE IN ATHENS

Cavafy

Who enters Lia's chamber? What bold young man
Approaching her luxuriant bed now offers
The haughty famous hetaera a spray of jasmine,
His outstretched hand revealing the gems on his fingers?

His tunic's made of the finest far-eastern silk,
Embroidered with an intricate scarlet pattern.
But even though his speech is pure Attic,
Still, the slightest accent of native Latin

Taints his flawless Greek with a trace of the Tiber.
Yet so intently does Lia the hetaera
Listen to Horace, her eloquent new lover,

You'd think the Athenian prostitute was a virgin
New to the language of erotic desire—
Spellbound as she is by the great Italian!

WITTGENSTEIN

He was good, as he said, at finding similes—
Certain things were alike, but words were different.
Proud that he'd not read a page of Aristotle,
But all of Street and Smith's Detective Stories.
No one of Jewish origins could be

Original, he yammered. But Yahweh was God.
Preferring, "on principle," Tolstoy's didactic essays,
He claimed he couldn't pick up, for the life of him,
The human pulse in Shakespeare, and why all the fuss.
The rules of logic were based on mistakes in grammar.

Three of his brothers committed suicide,
One a genius. Straight from the thick of the trenches
He got there a day too late to meet up with Trakl.
To follow philosophy was to lose your soul,
Especially if you had to lecture at Cambridge.

His lovers were few, their visits were brief, and sex
Was best when held at a passionate distance. At night
He'd whistle whole symphonies by heart—but only
Beethoven took his breath away. *Primordial
Life*, he wrote in his journal, *the wildness of life*

Erupting into the open—that's what I lack.
He gave up the richest trust fund in Austria
To teach at the village school in Otterthal.
The students were struck. One Josef Haidbauer
So hard on the head the sickly child passed out.

Herr Wittgenstein carried the boy to the principal's office,
And offered his resignation. In four years, at fourteen,
Haidbauer dies of cancer. Most insights took shape
During walks across a frozen lake, where the only
Norwegian neighbors in sight were those crystalline facets

Of ice at Skjolden, in pristine formulations.
A proposition is to be laid against
Reality like a ruler . . . When Ludwig went back
To apologize to the parents of his students
At Otterthal, the villagers rebuked him.

In his father's house there were seven grand pianos.

DAEDALOS

1

The Spartans claim their statue, "the oldest of Zeus,"
Is by Klearchos, pupil of Daedalos.

"Zeus the highest," in sheets of battered bronze
With bolts at the joints. But others insist it's by

Klearchos of Región, the student of Skyllus.
"Daedalos," as Peter Levi explains,

"Is a creature of primitive legend." On dumb dank walls
Of the Sibyl's cave, those murals of Daedalos.

And Virgil has verses that show how a skein unraveled
The labyrinth, blind turn by baffling turn.

Inside the heifer, cast in standing bronze,
Pasíphaë, the Queen, is down on all fours.

And mural by mural the Minotaur. And over
And over that ashen pair of open wings

Set down at the golden sandals of Phoebus Apollo.
And Daedalos himself, primordial maker,

Depicting himself in the act of suspending grief,
The chisel fallen free from his outstretched hands—

The father still trying to catch his falling son
Falling forever through all the brilliant skies

Of his spurious creation. And the tool falling too.

2

Even two years after the death of little Waldo,
Emerson said the loss had taught him nothing—

His fundamental nature remained unchanged.
"The reference of every kind of production"

(By which he also means reproduction, and art)
"Is at last to an aboriginal power." *Mammá,*

May I keep the bell I've made, by my bed? I'm afraid
It may alarm you, Mammá, if it rings too late

At night, and all of Concord wakes up to a sound
Louder than ten thousand hawks, Mammá, a noise

That crosses the water, to all the countries, like
Some great glass thing that falls and breaks to pieces.

3

My cousin Petro, young father, dying of cancer,
His countenance fixed, no matter how painful the chemo—

Until his children enter his hospital room.
Kneeling by the bed, his village father, Uncle

Leonidas, spreading his hands like Daedalos,
And calmly asking Christ what he did to deserve this.

Molón Labé is carved on Petro's headstone,
Along with a Spartan shield. "Come and take them."

Defiant words the doomed once aimed at Xerxes,
Whose messenger demanded: "Throw down your weapons!"

Molón Labé. "Come and take them." Moloch
Came and took him. *A father's no shield for his child.*

Swinging his censer back and forth on its chain,
Father Míhos thurified the grave, chanting

The Resurrection through wisps of dispersing smoke.
And then, at Woodlawn Cemetery, in Lynn,

Petro's mother, Aunt Efstathía, began
The ancient folk lament, the *mirologoi.*

Aunt Efstathía, lying facedown on the earth,
Screaming into the ground the name of her son,

Petro, begging the stones to take her to Petro.
Even the elders aghast, and no one knowing

How or when or if they should stop the keening.
The daughter's hand over her mouth, the priest kneeling.

And now my totally-out-of-it mother steps out
Of oblivion, as if part of a ritual

Too old to ever be touched by memory loss.
Ella, kaïménei. "Get up, wretch." And she does—

My aunt with the blades of grass on her long black dress,
My mother absentmindedly picking them off.

Embracing, they slap each other on the back
And across both shoulder blades, in that village way

Greek women show their mutual, hovering grief.
As if to say, to the dull thud of their backs

And shoulder blades: *it's here where the pinions should be,*
If we weren't human, and we could fly away.

4

The Spartans insist their statue, "the oldest of Zeus,"
Is by Klearchos, pupil of Daedalos.

But others cite Klearchos of Región,
The student of Skyllus. Daedalos, they claim,

Is a creature of primitive legend. *Zeus the Highest,*
Weeping from the clouds in tears of blood,

As Homer says, because the Fates had fixed
The fate of his son Sarpedon. The helpless sky-god

Encased in battered bronze, with bolts at the joints.
Clunky El Cid, the armor empty but still

Advancing its confabulated figment
Of ancient lament. Colossal Poundian phantoms.

Bogus then the king so steeped in dread
For his son the whole Aegean is named for the waves

Of agony that drowned poor Áegeus.
And fake the rock still called "The Calling Rock"—

As if an exhausted Deméter sat there calling
Persephone, Perseph . . . The boulder unmoved.

Even stone-faced Niobe, weeping for her nine children,
Nothing but forgeries of falling rain

Engraving the gouged cliff-face of Mount Sisyplos.
Look! There's Niobe, child, I hear my long-dead

Parents cry as we drive by the Quincy quarries.
And now I see it: that wild disfigured scree.

     5

The goddess Demeter, so devastated she sat
On a rock, exhausted. Aunt Efstathía in shock.

Emerson's blank bewilderment. They're like
The *daedala,* those figurines that are rendered

Almost as featureless as wooden blocks.
Pausanias saw one on the island of Naxos.

A tiny Aphrodite with broken arms.
He says the base was signed by Daedalos.

But where her flowing *peplos* should swirl at her feet
Diaphanous, he found *a four-square stump.*

On Naxos, where Ariadne was abandoned
By Theseus. Theseus, whose father was Áegeus,

Lord of precipitate dread. Ariadne, who threads
The monster's sinuous maze. The Labyrinth,

Synonymous now with the name of Daedalos—
Although it was only after he mastered the formal

Shapelessness of these wooden totemic figures
That Daedalos was given the title of *Maker.*

The reference of every kind of production
Is at last to an aboriginal power,

Emerson said, after losing his Icarus.
Expressionless, squat reliefs. Even older than

Picasso's Cycladic art. And not unlike
Those stark reliefs the Greek ambassador-poet

Brought back from the Dead Sea. It was during the war,
When George Seferis fled Damascus, and found

Himself on a rusting cargo ship, with refugees
Clutching their bundles. O shadowy depths of the hold,

Amorphous faces of fetishistic transport:
Daedala. We still don't know what they are.

BIRDS IN CEMETERIES

It must be the shade that draws them. Or else the grass.
And it seems they always alight away from their flocks,

Alone. It's so quiet here you can't help but hear
Their talons clink as they hop from headstone to headstone.

Their sharp, inquisitive beaks cast quizzical glances.
The lawn is mown. The gate is always open.

The names engraved on the stones, and the uplifting words
Below the names, are lapidary as ever.

But almost never even a chirp from the birds,
Let alone a wild shriek, as they perch on a tomb.

And then they fly away, looking as if
They couldn't remember why it was they came—

But were doing what our souls are supposed to do
On the day we die, if the birds could read the words.

ACKNOWLEDGMENTS

Poems in this book have appeared, some in slightly different versions, in the following publications:

Agni, Arion, Battery Journal, Berfrois, Charles River Journal, Consequence, Evergreen Review, Five Points, Free Inquiry, Hollow, Ibbetson Street, Literary Imagination, Literary Matters, Little Star, New Ohio Review, Paradise in Limbo, Poetry, Poetry Porch, Pusteblume, Salamander, and *Vergilius.*

My translation of Leopardi's poem "Saturday Night in the Village" is anthologized in *Joining Music with Reason: 34 Poets, British and American, Oxford 2004–2009,* edited by Christopher Ricks. It also appeared in my book of paired poems in translation, *Dialogos.*

"Spring" was translated into Greek by the Greek poet Maria Zervos and published in *Poeticanet.*

"Veil" was anthologized in *So Little Time: Words and Images for a World in Climate Change,* edited by Greg Delanty.

"The Funeral Oration" was anthologized in *Cities: Boston,* edited by Paul Rowe.

"Peponia" and "Reading ZH" were chosen for the Meringoff Prize for Poetry in 2014.

"Stele" appeared as a section of my poem "Hermes" in *Guide to Greece.*

"Hades" was chosen for the James Dickey Prize for Poetry in 2018.

"One-Credit Seminar on the Odes of Horace" is dedicated to Jonathan Aibel.

Various friends have been exacting and encouraging readers of these poems. I am especially grateful to Jonathan Aaron, Jonathan Aibel,

Jenny Barber, Daniel Bosch, Greg Delanty, Melissa Green, Katherine Jackson, Sarah Kafatou, Marcia Karp, Fred Marchant, Nicholas Racheotes, Ted Richer, Christopher Ricks, Dillon Tracy, Rosanna Warren, and Maria Zervos. And to James Long and Neal Novak, my patient and generous editors, my deepest appreciation.

CPSIA information can be obtained
at www.ICGtesting.com
Printed in the USA
LVHW091142021021
699302LV00005B/307

9 780807 175675